LARRY BIRD

Hall of Fame Basketball Superstar

Jack Kavanagh

Speeding Star, an imprint of Enslow Publishers, Inc.

Library of Congress Cataloging-in-Publication Data
Kavanagh, Jack.
  Larry Bird : hall of fame basketball superstar / Jack Kavanagh.
      p. cm. — (Hall of fame sports greats)
  Rev. ed. of Sports great Larry Bird.
  Includes bibliographical references and index.
  Summary: "Learn about the life of Hall of Fame basketball player Larry Bird in this sports biography.
From all of the struggles and hardships he faced as a child, Larry found a way to overcome it all and be-
come one of the best basketball players in Boston Celtics' and NBA history"—Provided by publisher.
  ISBN 978-1-62285-030-3
  1. Bird, Larry, 1956- —Juvenile literature. 2. Basketball players—United States—Biography—
Juvenile literature. 3. Boston Celtics (Basketball team)—Juvenile literature. I. Kavanagh, Jack.
Sports great Larry Bird. II. Title.
  GV884.B57K37 2013
  796.323092--dc23
  [B]

                                   2012050548

Paperback ISBN: 978-1-62285-031-0   EPUB ISBN: 978-1-62285-033-4
Single-User PDF ISBN: 978-1-62285-034-1   Multi-User PDF ISBN: 978-1-62285-149-2

Printed in the United States of America
062013 Lake Book Manufacturing, Inc., Melrose Park, IL
10 9 8 7 6 5 4 3 2 1

To Our Readers: We have done our best to make sure all Internet addresses in this book were active
and appropriate when we went to press. However, the author and the Publisher have no control over,
and assume no liability for, the material available on those Internet sites or on other Web sites they may
link to. Any comments or suggestions can be sent by e-mail to comments@speedingstar.com or to the
following address:

Speeding Star
Box 398, 40 Industrial Road
Berkeley Heights, NJ 07922
USA
www.speedingstar.com

Photo Credits: AP Images, pp. 17, 27, 47, 52, 58; AP Images/Brian Horten, p. 22; AP Images/Dar-
ron Cummings, p. 14; AP Images/Elise Amendola, pp. 4, 40; AP Images/G. Paul Burnett, p. 36; AP
Images/Jerome McLendon, p. 25; AP Images/Kennedy, p. 44; AP Images/Liss, p. 29; AP Images/Mar-
tell, p. 10; AP Images/Matthew Cavanaugh, p. 60; AP Images/Paul R. Benoit, p. 8; AP Images/Peter
Southwick, pp. 1, 19, 54; AP Images/Steve Pyle, pp. 33, 38.

Cover Photo: AP Images/Peter Southwick

This title was originally published in 1992 as *Sports Great Larry Bird*.

CONTENTS

Larry Bird has his hands up to defend the shot of Julius Erving. Bird and Erving (also known as Dr. J) had many epic battles throughout their careers.

Chapter 1

Plenty to Celebrate

Larry Bird had never heard the fans shout "We're Number One!" Not in high school, not in college, and, up to this time, not as a Celtic. Larry had never played on a state or national championship team. He had been a star player in high school and college. His teams had been eliminated in the final round in two championship tournaments—first in high school and next in college. In his second season as a professional player, Larry Bird got another chance to play for a championship.

The 1980–81 regular season ended with the Boston Celtics tied with the previous year's National Basketball Association (NBA) champions. The Philadelphia 76ers and the Boston Celtics had each won 62 games and lost 20. Now they had to battle it out in the Eastern Conference Finals. Whichever team won would meet the Western Conference playoff winner. That series would decide the NBA championship.

Philadelphia won three of the first four games. It looked bad for Bird and the Celtics. One more Sixers' win and it was all over. Philadelphia even led 109-103 in the fifth game with just 90 seconds to play. But the Celtics snatched the victory by running off eight points while holding the Sixers scoreless.

Even so, it still seemed to be a lost cause for Boston. The next game would be played in Philadelphia, and the Celtics had lost their last 11 games at the Spectrum. The noisy Sixers fans made it tough on visiting teams. Yet, even though the Celtics fell behind by 17 points, they caught up with two seconds left to play. Cedric Maxwell put in two free throws for a 100-98 Celtics' win. The series was tied, and the teams would go back to Boston to settle matters.

However, it was the Sixers who led all the way until late in the final quarter of the deciding game. They were ahead by six points when Larry Bird took over. He stole a pass from the great Sixers forward Julius Erving. Bird then whipped the ball to Tiny Archibald, who was fouled. Archibald sank both free throws. Next Bird picked off another Sixer pass. He fed it to Robert Parish, who tossed in a turnaround jumper. Then Larry Bird was fouled by Julius Erving and calmly swished two free throws through the net. The score was tied at 89-89.

With only seconds to play, Erving drove for a layup, but Larry leaped high and swatted the ball away. When another Sixer, Darryl Dawkins, swooped in for a layup, he missed, and

Larry came down with the rebound. He took off along the left sideline, dribbling toward the basket. Then he stopped, took aim, and banked in the tiebreaker for a 91-89 Celtics lead. The game ended seconds later with Boston winning by one-point, 91-90.

Larry Bird told the reporters who crowded into the Celtics' dressing room, "I wanted to take the last shot." When the game is on the line, Larry Bird always wants the job of winning it.

With the dangerous Sixers eliminated, the NBA final round was expected to be easy for the Celtics. The winner of the Western Conference was Houston. Boston had beaten the Rockets the last thirteen times the two teams met. However, the Celtics were in for a letdown after their furious battles with the Sixers. They opened in the Boston Garden, but Houston led all the way. Finally, Larry Bird made what Celtics general manager Red Auerbach, of the 1960 and 1970s, called "the greatest play I have ever seen." After his 18-foot shot bounced off the rim, Larry raced in for the rebound. As he flew through the air, he shifted the ball to his left hand. Just before he crashed among the photographers along the baseline, he flipped the ball toward the basket, and it went in. The Boston fans were on their feet. The hard-charging Celtics ran off eight points, and Larry sank a final layup with 19 seconds to go. That gave Boston a 98-95 win in Game 1.

The NBA championship series was not over yet. Houston won two of the next three games. Larry Bird was in a rare shooting slump. He did what he always did when that happened. He made up for it with other parts of his game. He

Larry Bird elevates to the rim in a game against the Houston Rockets.

led both teams in assists and steals and battled Moses Malone, Houston's star, to a draw in rebounds. Even without Bird's usual point total, the team play of the Celtics brought them a 109-80 win in the Game 5. They needed one more victory to become champions, and Larry's slump ended in Game 6. He scored 27 points, getting the critical ones in the final minutes. The Houston Rockets did not give up easily. Three times in the last minutes they came within three points of the lead. Each time the Rockets got close, Larry Bird stopped them. He hit on a 15-foot jumper. Then he lobbed a pass to Cedric Maxwell for a three-pointer from beyond the 26-foot circle. Finally he added his own three-pointer to put the game on ice. Boston won 102-91. The Celtics were NBA champs for the fourteenth time, but for Larry Bird it was his first.

Larry Bird, the greatest all-around player in NBA history according to many experts, had not been a "one man gang." Just the opposite was true. He has always been a dedicated team player. The NBA title was a team championship. His accurate passes to teammates led to points being scored. They counted just as much as those he personally put in the basket. Of all the statistics, assists is by far the most important to Larry Bird.

Over the years, Red Auerbach had become known for his "victory cigar" after Boston Celtics' triumphs. When a critical game was won, he would "light up." The happy Larry Bird snatched Red's cigar and took a few puffs himself. He had plenty to celebrate.

When the Celtics arrived back in Boston, they were paraded through the city's crowded streets. Larry waved to more people

Bird waves to the crowd during the Celtics victory parade after winning the 1980–81 NBA championship.

than he had ever seen before in his life. They cheered him and his Celtics teammates. Larry Bird now played on the best basketball team in the world. Back in Indiana, it had been Larry's fate to be the best player on a team from a small-town high school. In college he had dropped out of Indiana University, a national powerhouse, and went to the much smaller Indiana State. Even when he joined the Boston Celtics, a team that had won more championships than any other professional basketball team, they had become losers. The year before Larry Bird joined them, the Celtics won only 29 games and lost 53. The next season, with Bird taking charge, they won 61 and lost only 21. They improved by an incredible 32 games. They lost in the Eastern Conference Finals to Philadelphia, 4–1, that first year.

For the 1980–81 season the Celtics added two key players. Robert Parish, a 7-foot center, and Kevin McHale, a 6-foot 10-inch forward, were able to control the ball under the basket. Along with Cedric Maxwell, Tiny Archibald, M. L. Carr, and Chris Ford, Coach Bill Fitch was able to put together a team for Larry Bird to lead to victory.

In the TD Garden, where the Celtics play their home games, championship banners are hung from the rafters. Each lists a year when the Boston Celtics won the NBA championship. There are 17 banners hanging high above the floor. The first was won in 1957, when the NBA had just eight teams. There were only four teams in each division. Today there are 30 teams and six divisions. In the early years there were fewer teams to beat, and the playoffs were much shorter. The Celtics won the championship eight years straight, from 1959 to 1966. That was the time when the immortal Bill Russell was the dominant player on the Celtics. For many years he has been considered one of the greatest players of all time. Red Auerbach, who coached Russell, always insisted that Russell was the best player of all time. Finally, even Auerbach had to concede that as great as Russell had been, Larry Bird was the better all-around player. There are fewer championship banners hanging from the rafters of the Boston Garden from the Bird era than from the Russell era. Bird's Celtics won three times, while Russell's Celtics won eleven championships. But in Bird's time the schedules became longer, and the teams became better balanced. The rules had been changed to reduce the "home-court advantage," which used to favor the division winners.

What counted most with Larry Bird was that he was a champion at last. As the team's leader, he could have told the people of Boston the victory was dedicated to them. Instead, he remembered how disappointed his friends and neighbors had been when tiny Springs Valley High School had failed to win the Indiana high school state championship in 1975. Larry Bird made a point of dedicating his share of that Celtics victory to the folks back home. Then he said good-bye to Boston. He went home to where he lived between basketball seasons, the rural community of French Lick, Indiana.

Basketball Consumed Him

If some babies are born to grow up to become basketball players, Larry Bird fits the description. He was born on December 7, 1956. There were three older children, but none had come into the world the size of their baby brother, Larry Joe. He weighed 11 pounds, 12 ounces, and was 23 inches long. His parents were of Irish and Scottish descent, and there was American Indian blood on both sides.

The blond-haired infant was doing push-ups when he was three months old and walked alone when he was nine months old. In his first year he had torn apart several cribs and a playpen. After that, he shared a regular bed with his older brothers, Mike and Mark.

Georgia Kerns married Joe Bird on September 20, 1951. She was twenty-one, and the tallest of seven children. The large Kerns family was poor. Almost everyone in the region was. The Birds, who had an even bigger family, were even worse off than most of their neighbors. Larry's father, Joe Bird, had been a great athlete as a teenager but never even played high school sports. He enlisted in the United States Navy in 1944, when he was eighteen, and saw battle action in the Pacific. He was restless when the war ended, and in 1951 he joined the army for the Korean War. He was a combat infantryman and came home with terrible nightmares. These would severely disturb him for the rest of his life.

The Bird and Kerns families were typical of the people who

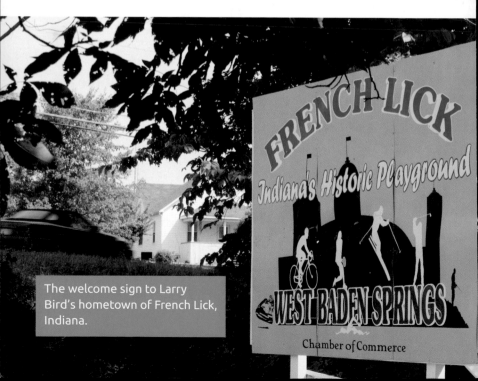

The welcome sign to Larry Bird's hometown of French Lick, Indiana.

lived in Orange County. It was the poorest county in southern Indiana. A lot of kids dropped out of school, and very few ever went to college. Many left the area to look for better-paying jobs. Those who stayed behind farmed, did odd jobs, or worked in small factories. French Lick had once been a famous health resort. Wealthy people came to use the natural hot springs. The water was bottled and shipped around the world. The resort industry employed many local people. During World War II, when travel restrictions prevented Major League Baseball teams from going south for spring training, the Chicago Cubs got ready for the 1944 and 1945 seasons in French Lick. Then the big resorts closed and the local people lost their jobs. To make ends meet, Georgia Bird worked two jobs to bring in $100 a week. But it cost $125 to feed the family.

Joe Bird went from job to job, making good money as a furniture finisher, but his paycheck rarely came home with him on payday. He would spend his money in bars before he ever got home to his family.

Larry Bird grew up in a troubled family. His grandmother, Lizzie Kerns, though, was a gentle and caring woman who helped Georgia raise her many children. After Larry was born, two more boys joined the family. Larry was a particular favorite of his grandmother and lived at her house more than he did in his own home. The Birds moved often, unable to pay the rent. They would take their furniture to one ramshackle house after another. One thing that always went along was the basketball hoop that was nailed up behind the house. After Larry Bird became a professional basketball player, he built his mother a house. He filled it with new furniture. This time, they did not move the old basketball hoop. Instead, Larry had a regulation basketball court built beside the new house.

There was a lot of love among the Birds. Christmas was always made special, even if money had to be borrowed to buy toys. The first gift Larry remembers getting was a basketball. He left it behind the wood-burning stove Christmas night, and in the morning it was covered with bumps and no longer round. It did not matter to Larry. He carried it with him everywhere.

Larry's older brothers, Mike and Mark, set the pace for Larry to become an athlete. They made their kid brother pitch batting practice and chase down basketballs. Larry grew up like other youngsters in the rough environment of French Lick and the nearby towns. Sports, hunting and fishing, and just hanging out were what kids did. Years later, when Larry Bird locked the door of his expensive home in Boston at the end of the season, those were the things he did in the offseason.

Larry learned from his brothers that he had to keep up with his schoolwork so he could play on the athletic teams. Mark and Mike both played sports for the district high school. Mike was the best and went on to college. When Larry made the high school varsity team, he was given number 33. It had been his brother Mike's number. He had worn that number ever since. In college and in the NBA, Larry Bird was number 33. When he ended his playing career, the Boston Celtics retired his uniform number. They also have back at Indiana State and Springs Valley High School.

Larry was good at all sports. He might have become a great

When Larry made his high school basketball team, he was given No. 33. It was the same number his older brother, Mike, had worn. Larry would wear No. 33 for the rest of his career. In this photo, Red Auerbach is giving Bird his first Celtics jersey.

quarterback. The way he passes a basketball the length of the court gives an idea of how good he could have been. He always played games with older boys so he could test his developing skills. He played the outfield and shortstop in baseball. One year they made up a team just of the Bird brothers and their cousins, and Larry was the best player they had.

But basketball was his first choice. It consumed him. He

played endlessly. He rode his bike to any place there was a game. If there were not enough players for a regular game, they would use half the court and play three on a side. If that could not be done, he would shoot baskets with another boy. They would take turns chasing rebounds. If no one else showed up, Larry would take his shots and go after the ball himself. As long as there was a basket and a ball, Larry would practice. Throughout his career he was always the first player in the gym and the last to leave. Constant practice was Larry's trademark. It is the reason he improved each season. His shooting average improved even after he became an all-star.

Larry developed slowly on the high school team. Even though he practiced endlessly, he was not a star at first. Then during his junior year, he became tall enough to dominate in high school competition. Over one summer he grew six inches. Suddenly he was 6 feet 9 inches, and Coach Gary Holland switched him to center.

Even so, in Indiana it is hard to get recognition when you play for a school in a small town. High school basketball is almost a religion in the state. Basketball was invented in western Massachusetts by Dr. James Naismith in the winter of 1891–92. He was a teacher at the YMCA College in Springfield. His graduates took the game with them when they went to work at YMCAs in other states. Indiana was the first state outside of Massachusetts to take up basketball. It was the perfect game for a state with many small farming towns. There was great rivalry, especially in sports, between the towns. Basketball was made-to-order for them. The season started right after the fall harvest

Practice pays off for those who work hard. As a young man, Bird was constantly working on his game. Larry is shown here blocking a shot by Gerald Wilkins of the New York Knicks.

and went on until spring planting. High school gyms held more people than lived in town.

Larry was injured as a sophomore, so he did not really develop as a player until his junior year. As a senior, he led the state of Indiana in scoring. He averaged over 30 points a game. He scored 55 points in one game and pulled down 38 rebounds in another. Larry became a real leader. He got his teammates to the gym at 6:30 in the morning to practice shooting fouls. It almost paid off when Springs Valley just missed winning its regional tournament. However, the one boy who had always skipped early morning practice missed four free throws in a row at the end of the final game. The fans of the high school team were disappointed. However, they looked forward to Larry Bird's college career.

From College to the Celtics

Even before his team made the state finals, Larry Bird had been spotted by Bobby Knight, head coach at Indiana University. The folks of French Lick, Larry's hometown, were excited. The best players were at Indiana University. Larry was not sure he was ready to go to a big university. There were 30,000 students. He was only seventeen years old. He had never been out of the state except to play in a tournament. He was on the all-star Indiana squad when they played the Kentucky boys at Louisville.

Larry Bird finally accepted the scholarship offer to Indiana University. He reached the Bloomington campus for preseason practice, but in less than a month he went home. The coach,

After an unpleasant semester at Indiana University, Larry Bird transferred to Indiana State University, where he became a college star.

Bobby Knight, gave him no help. Larry roomed with another boy whose family had money. His clothes filled the closets in the room. Larry owned only a few extra pair of blue jeans, some T-shirts, and the suit he had worn to his high school graduation. Discouraged and lonely, the seventeen- year-old suddenly went home. Back in French Lick, many people were disappointed when Larry left college. When the greatest basketball player ever to come out of Springs Valley High School took a job working on a garbage truck, they felt let down.

It was not until a year later that Larry Bird went back to college. This time he went to the much smaller Indiana State University. He lost a year of eligibility to play intercollegiate basketball because he changed schools. By 1975, Larry Bird's life had changed in other ways. His parents had divorced, and then his father died. Soon after he enrolled at Indiana State, Larry married his high school girlfriend, Janet Condra. It did not last long. Yet, after the divorce, Larry learned he was the father of a daughter named Corrie. Bird would not become a big part of her life.

Basketball became even more important to Larry. When he was not in class, he was in the gym. He practiced over and over, always improving his game. He could not play on the Indiana State team during the 1975–76 season. They had a 12–12 record. The next year the Sycamores lost only three games. Once Larry was eligible to play, they jumped to a 25–3 record in 1976–77. He averaged 33 points and 13 rebounds a game.

The next year, Indiana State won 23 games while Larry averaged 30 points a game. He had one more year to play college basketball. However, because he had lost a year of eligibility when he dropped out of Indiana University, the NBA could draft him. When the Boston Celtics claimed him, Larry had a problem. He needed money. However, he had told his mother he would be the first in the family to graduate from college. Boston would have to wait. Larry played his final year at Indiana State University.

What a year it was! Bird led all college players in scoring. Indiana State went through its schedule without losing a game. They won the Missouri Valley Conference title. They were No. 1 there, but it only gave them a place in the big National Collegiate Athletic Association postseason tournament. The NCAA is the real test for college teams. Indiana State rolled right along. They ran their winning streak to 33 games and reached the Final Four.

Bird scored 35 points to edge out DePaul in a semifinal game, 76–74. Next came the biggest test. Larry Bird and Indiana State would meet Magic Johnson and Michigan State. Both players were 6 feet, 9 inches. Larry played forward, and Magic was a superstar at guard. Magic came from a big city; Lansing, Michigan. Larry was from a small rural community. Magic is black, and Larry is white. At the time, it might have mattered to some people but not to the two players. In their first meeting in the Final Four, they learned to respect each other's basketball ability. After both had become stars in the NBA, their natural rivalry grew into warm admiration for each other. Magic visited Larry in French Lick. They have many things in common beyond great basketball ability. Larry is one

Larry Bird (right) and Earvin "Magic" Johnson (left) meet prior to their showdown in the 1979 NCAA Championship Game.

of six children, and Magic has nine sisters and brothers. Larry's parents both worked hard. Magic's dad held two jobs to keep his family together. Larry Bird and Magic Johnson are very much alike. Both hold family values in high esteem. Each had considered the other the best player in the NBA. They were both been voted Most Valuable Player in the NBA three times. Either Bird or Johnson was the MVP six times in seven seasons, 1984 through 1990.

Magic Johnson and Michigan State ended Indiana State's unbeaten streak, 75–64. They double-teamed Bird and held him to 19 points. He had averaged 28.6 during the season. However, Larry was named College Basketball Player of the Year for 1978–79. He was headed for the NBA and so was Magic Johnson. Larry Bird went back to Terre Haute, where Indiana State is located, and graduated in June. He was eager to start his professional basketball career.

Larry Bird left for Boston armed with good advice. Four leading businessmen in Terre Haute formed The Committee. They helped Larry find the best agent to handle his contract with the Celtics. Bob Woolf, an attorney who represented many top stars, was the one Larry picked. When Larry moved to Boston, he bought a house next door to Bob Woolf's house. Larry and his girlfriend, Dinah Mattingly, became close friends of Bob and Annie Woolf and their children. Larry had always been lucky to have wise and experienced people around him, and he has been smart enough to listen to them. The millions of dollars he has earned have been wisely invested. He has been

Celtics president Red Auerbach and Larry Bird were all smiles during the press conference announcing that Bird had signed with Boston.

free to concentrate on being the greatest basketball player he can be.

Larry checked in at the Celtics rookie camp and began his career in pro basketball. The fans and the press had already welcomed him. They expected that he would lead the Celtics back to the top of the NBA. It was different when Larry met his new teammates. They would make him prove how good he was.

The player who tested Larry the hardest was Cedric Maxwell. He was the key player on the Celtics and proud of it. He wanted Larry Bird to make good. Everyone would play better if Larry lived up to expectations. That is the way it worked out. When the Celtics won their next NBA title, Cedric Maxwell was the MVP in the playoffs.

Larry also had to show his new coach, Bill Fitch, that he would learn to play "the Celtics' way." It did not take long. As always, Bird was the first to arrive for practice and the last to leave. He passed the ball to any teammate who had a better shot. He hurried back down the court quickly on defense. It was clear that he had great talent. What the coach and the other players also liked was his great attitude. He was a "team player."

Larry Bird's first test as a professional came in an exhibition game. The Boston Celtics and the Philadelphia 76ers were traditional rivals. The Sixers were heavily favored when the teams met at Madison Square Garden in New York City. Larry would play against the most exciting player in basketball. Julius Erving had led the way to a new style of playing. It depended on speed and great leaping ability. Erving, who was called Dr. J., seemed to hang in the air when he went up for a shot. Bird came from the traditional style of play. The idea was to be patient. You moved the ball around until someone got open. A well-placed shot by Larry Bird swishes through the strings of the net. Players like Dr. J. score their points with a slam dunk that rattles the backboard.

The preseason game would not count in the standings. However, Madison Square Garden was jammed with fans.

Bird gets ready to practice before a day of Celtics rookie camp.

Reporters from everywhere covered the game. It was the start of the Bird Era. People wanted to know if the Celtics would once again become NBA champions. Larry's job was to guard Julius Erving. He did it well, although the Sixers beat the Celtics easily, 115-90. However, Bird had passed his first test. The reporters crowded the dressing rooms of both teams after the game. They wanted to know what Julius Erving thought of the new kid on the block. Dr. J. told them, "He can play. He moves real good. You can feel his intensity. I am very favorably impressed with him as a player."

Larry said he was glad it was over. "When the game started, all I could think of was stopping Julius Erving. I wasn't thinking about my offense at all." Erving had missed his first three shots, and Bird played the rest of the game with great confidence.

The Boston Celtics opened the 1979–80 season at home. The Boston Garden was packed with fans. They hoped that Bird would prove how good he was. The Houston Rockets were a real test. They were led by Moses Malone, the previous year's MVP. He was a center and dominated the action under the backboards.

The Celtics lived up to the hopes of their fans. They not only won, 114-106, but they also played as a team. Some were veterans of past seasons, and others had come in trades. Bird was the only rookie in the lineup. In the season's opener, his aggressive play got him into foul trouble. He played only 28 minutes. He scored a respectable 14 points. He also grabbed 10 rebounds and had 5 assists to do his share in winning the game.

It did not take long for the Celtics to show they were back

on track. They won 15 of their first 20 games. They played with the tight-knit teamwork of past Celtics teams. It was clear that Larry Bird made the difference. Just as Cedric Maxwell had hoped, Bird made his teammates better players. It had been the same in high school and college. While Bird lacked the speed and jumping ability of most NBA forwards, he made up for his shortcomings by anticipating. He had exceptional vision. He seemed to know where everyone was on the court. He sensed what they were about to do. Bird acted on this instinct smartly. His passes led teammates who then scored on easy layups. He stepped into the other team's passing lanes and stole the ball. As Red Auerbach explained after Bird won the Rookie of the Year honors, "Larry never was really a rookie. He played like a veteran from the start."

The Second Title

The Boston Celtics began a new dynasty for the 1980s, the Bird Era. Boston was back in the playoffs at the end of Larry Bird's first season. The next season Larry would lead the Celtics all the way to the NBA championship. After that, the question became, "Could they win back-to-back NBA titles?" It had not been done since the pre-Bird Celtics did it in 1968 and 1969.

The team added Danny Ainge to the backcourt. Ainge once passed up professional basketball to play big-league baseball with the Toronto Blue Jays. After a few subpar seasons, he switched back to basketball, and the Celtics had him. Young Danny Ainge would take the pressure off the Celtics' older

Looking through the defense, Bird gets ready to pass to Celtics teammate Danny Ainge.

guards. He was a deadly three-point shooter and an exciting ball handler. Like Larry Bird, he could use either hand equally well. They both wrote and ate left-handed, but controlled the ball with the right hand. Players who are ambidextrous can pass or score by using either hand when necessary.

Although they were the defending champs and seemed even stronger, the Celtics started slowly. Then Larry Bird got hot. He had two triple doubles in three nights. This term is usually used when a player has double figures for points, assists, and rebounds. The Celtics ran up a new team winning streak. They won 18 in a row. Then Larry took a vicious elbow to the face. He lay motionless for a long time before being helped to the locker room. Bird got back into the game and even slam-dunked the winning points to beat the league-leading Milwaukee Bucks, 106-102. Then X-rays taken after the game showed he had a fractured cheekbone. Larry could not play. When he came back, he played as the sixth man. This is the first player off the bench. He played less time than usual but substituted in key situations. Only a dedicated team player could do such a thing. It resulted in a Celtics' season record of 63–19.

Larry's own stats had improved over the previous season. He was named to the All-NBA First Team. On January 31 he had won the MVP award in the All-Star Game. An NBA title would have capped a great season, but it was not to be. In the second round, the Celtics met their usual rival, the Philadelphia 76ers. The series went the full seven games, but when the Celtics' playmaker, Tiny Archibald, was hurt in the third game,

Boston went flat. Bird could not will the team to win. He had never completely regained his best form after his own injury.

After a typical summer back in Indiana, where his injuries healed, Larry Bird was ready for the 1982–83 season. Again the team seemed improved. Quinn Buckner, another Indiana native who had starred at Indiana University, joined the team. However, the Sixers signed all-star center Moses Malone, the reigning league MVP.

Bird got off to the greatest start of his career and carried the Celtics with him. Yet when their record stood at 18–4, they were tied with Philadelphia. The Los Angeles Lakers in the other division were also 18–4. It was to be that kind of season. The two top teams in the East were matching each other, and whichever won could expect to take on the Lakers for the NBA championship.

Professional athletes rarely risk "calling the shot." Babe Ruth did it once in a World Series. He said he would hit a home run and did it. Larry did something of the sort at Phoenix on February 26. He was playing on a badly sprained ankle. There was one second left in a game the Celtics were losing 101–100. The Phoenix Suns counted their chickens too soon. One player taunted Bird that they would stop him on the last play of the game. Larry answered back by saying he would personally score the winning basket. The ball was in-bounded to Bird, who took it with his back to the basket far beyond the three-point line. He whirled and shot … swish! Larry ran off the court laughing.

On March 30, Bird set a new Celtics single-game scoring record of 53 points. The Celtics were playing winning

Larry Bird eyes a loose ball during the 1982 NBA All-Star Game. He was named the game's MVP.

basketball. But the Sixers, with Moses Malone, were five games ahead of them. Boston began to let down and ended with a 56–26 record. It was the first time they had won less than 60 games since the "Bird Era" began.

The Celtics played badly in the playoffs. They did not have to worry about Philadelphia. The Milwaukee Bucks knocked the Celtics out of the playoffs in the second round in four straight. The blame was placed on Coach Bill Fitch. The team's morale was very low. Everyone was relieved when K. C. Jones was named head coach for the coming season. He had been an assistant coach and had been a great Celtics player. Bird went home determined to improve his game even more. He practiced on the court beside his mother's house. He ran three or four miles a day. He thought hard about what could be done to help the Celtics return to the top of the NBA.

Once again, the smart general manager, Red Auerbach, had swung a deal to improve the Celtics. The 1983–84 team added point guard Dennis Johnson. He had been named to the NBA's All-Defensive team the past five seasons, playing with Phoenix and Seattle. He mixed very well with the Celtics' veterans, particularly with Larry Bird.

One thing the Celtics had lacked at the end of the last season was a fighting spirit. Bird set out to show the rest of the league how tough Boston was. The exhibition season opened in the Boston Garden against their old enemy, the Philadelphia 76ers. Last year, after the Celtics had been eliminated, the Sixers had won the championship. On top of that, Moses Malone was once again voted the league's MVP. The Sixers set out to

Larry Bird knocks over Milwaukee Bucks defender Junior Bridgeman on his way to the basket during the second round of the 1983 Eastern Conference playoffs. The Bucks swept the series in four straight games.

physically intimidate the Celtics right there on their home court. The game had just begun when Moses Malone tackled Cedric Maxwell. Max threw the ball at him. Less than a minute later, Bird cut himself in on the action. He and Mark Iavaroni grabbed each other's shirt. Bird hit the big man in the mouth and went after the even bigger Malone. Most brawls between athletes are just pushing and shoving matches. The players have never learned how to fight. Bird came from the hardscrabble country of southern Indiana. Boys grew up fighting to hang on to the few things they owned. Bird was a devastating battler.

Before the melee was over, Red Auerbach had his glasses off and was in Malone's face out on the floor. Red and Larry drew big fines from the NBA, but they had made their point. No one was going to push the Celtics around this season. The Boston Celtics romped through the schedule. By the end of January, they had won 35 and lost only 9 games. They ended with 62 victories—the best record in the league. They expected to meet the Sixers in the final round of the Eastern Conference playoffs. Instead, Philadelphia was knocked out by the New Jersey Nets. The Celtics' toughest challenge would come from the New York Knicks.

Bernard King was the fabulous star of the Knicks. It seemed certain that either he or Bird would be voted MVP for the season. The momentum in the playoff series swung back and forth. Finally it came to a seventh game in Boston. The series had been furiously fought. There had been ten technical fouls called. There were three ejections and one bench-clearing brawl. Larry Bird finally settled things by playing the finest

Bird has to be restrained by teammates after getting into a fight with Mark Iavaroni of the Philadelphia 76ers. This happened during a preseason game in October 1983.

playoff game of his career. He had 28 points at the end of the first half. That was more than Bernard King would score in the whole game. He ended the third quarter with a three-pointer. Bird outplayed King in every phase of the game. For the series, he averaged 30.4 points, 10.6 rebounds, and 7.1 assists. He shot 58.5 percent and sank 90 percent of his foul shots.

The Celtics were out to avenge their four straight losses to Milwaukee in the prior year's playoffs. The Celtics wiped out the Bucks in five games. They were back in the NBA Finals for the first time in three years.

It would be Larry Bird against Magic Johnson once more. That's the way the public viewed it. Both players saw it differently. Magic and Larry played different positions. The Celtics counted on Larry Bird to score most of the team's points. Kareem Abdul-Jabbar, a Hall-of-Fame center, was the Lakers' main scoring threat. Magic Johnson's role was passing and defense.

The Celtics were almost wiped out in four straight games. Only a bad play by the Lakers made a Celtics win possible in Game 2. In Game 4, Larry Bird rallied his team, almost coming to blows with Abdul-Jabbar. With 16 seconds left to play, Bird tied the score. The game went to overtime. Then Bird made a game-winning 16-foot turnaround shot. The series was tied at two games each.

Game 5, at the old Boston Garden, gave the Celtics a unique home-court advantage. The air conditioning broke down, and it was 97 degrees on the court. The Lakers could hardly breathe. It did not bother Larry. He hit on 15 of 20 shots and had 17 rebounds. He scored 34 points and outlasted everyone on the floor. The series went back to the West Coast. Once more the Lakers tied the series. Once again it would take a seventh game to decide the NBA title. Back in Boston, the Celtics won their fifteenth NBA title. It was their second in the "Bird Era." Larry was named NBA Finals MVP, as well as the regular season MVP for the first time. He was at the peak of his career.

Before he went home for the summer, Bird did a very nice thing. The Celtics had an elderly equipment man. He had been with the team since the first NBA season, 1949–50. Bird told the other Celtics he wanted to buy Walter Randall a championship ring. No one had ever done anything like this. It made the last year of Walter's life happier. He died of cancer during the next season.

Larry Bird was not a player who would rest on his laurels. He kept motivating himself to improve year after year. Bird saw the coming 1984–85 season as another challenge.

Three-Time Champ

The Celtics began the new season where they had left off. They won steadily. Larry was hot, and the Sixers were again the team to beat. Even with Moses Malone, Philadelphia's main man was still Julius Erving. He and Larry Bird were head-to-head rivals. The first meeting of the new season ended in a pushing match. Larry outscored Dr. J. 42 points to 6, and Erving did not like it. Both players were fined $7,500. People joked that the two rivals could pay with the money they made doing TV commercials together. They were friends off the court, but neither wanted to be second best when they played each other.

The Celtics seemed to be even better than the year before. They ran off long winning streaks. Games often ended with

Larry Bird guards Julius Erving during a game in 1980. The men were fierce competitors on the court, but friends off the court.

a spectacular shot by Larry Bird. Portland, for example, was about to beat the Celtics in the Boston Garden. Only one second remained with the Trail Blazers ahead, 128–127. Bird took a downcourt pass in the left corner. With two players all over him, he shot as he fell out of bounds. The ball went high in the air. It passed over a corner of the backboard and fell through the net for another impossible victory.

Injuries are part of the long NBA season. Celtics forward Cedric Maxwell blew out his knee. Kevin McHale became a starter to stay. He broke Bird's Celtics single-game scoring record of 53. McHale got 56 on March 3. Nine days later, Bird reclaimed the record. He tossed in 60 points against the Atlanta Hawks. Then an injury caught up with Bird. His elbow, banged hard so many times when he dove for loose balls, hurt badly. He could play, but it was painful to shoot.

The Celtics made quick work of Cleveland to open the 1984–85 playoffs. Next were the Detroit Pistons. Bird had several great games and some bad ones, but the Celtics won. He took off the protective elbow pad and got ready for the conference finals against the familiar rivals, the Philadelphia 76ers. The Celtics won in five games when Bird stole the ball with four seconds to play. It saved a 102–100 victory. However, the stat sheets showed that Bird was not scoring his usual numbers. Against Detroit his shooting average fell below his season average. Against Philadelphia he dropped even farther. His elbow still hurt, and he played the Sixers with a bandaged finger.

The Los Angeles Lakers were favored in the final round.

Bird was slowed down by a chronic bad back, plus his elbow and finger problems. As a result, the Celtics were the underdogs. Amazingly, they trounced the Lakers 148–114 in the opener. Then a Kareem elbow added a bloody nose to Larry's list of injuries. Still, the Celtics fought on. In Game 4, Boston was in danger of falling behind three games to one. The Celtics trailed 92–85 with less than 10 minutes to play. Bird's eight unanswered points put the Celtics in the lead temporarily. With 12 seconds left, the score was tied. The Lakers looked for Bird to take the final shot. He crossed them up. He spotted Dennis Johnson wide open. D. J. hit a 20-footer just ahead of the buzzer. That was it for the Celtics, however. Larry shot badly, the team lost the next two, and the Lakers wrapped up the title. Bird still took one trophy back to Indiana. He was voted regular-season MVP for the second straight time.

The 1985–86 season would be another great one for Bird and the Celtics. Red Auerbach had worked another of his surprise additions to the team. He traded Cedric Maxwell for the one-time superstar, center Bill Walton. He had been the MVP back in 1977–78 and had led the Portland Trail Blazers to the NBA championship the season before. Then he had to give up the game. He had stress fractures in his feet that would not heal. Walton had reconstructive surgery and missed a couple seasons. Now he was with the Celtics. They hoped he could give them 20 minutes a game—long enough to rest Robert Parish.

Larry Bird played far below his usual form when the season began. His chronic back problem slowed him down. Then he found a trainer who had helped other athletes get back into

The 1985–86 Celtics team is honored as the championship banner is hung in the old Boston Garden.

action. Dan Dyrek got Bird into shape to play again. He was back in form for the All-Star Game. For the first time, the game featured a three-point shooting match. The eight best players in the NBA at sinking long shots were invited. They would have 60 seconds to get off 25 shots. Larry loved it. It was like being back in an Indiana gym and being challenged by his friends. One winning strategy was to "psych out" the others. Bird asked them, "Since my name is already on the check, which of you is going to get second-place money?" He had another way to upset his competition. When the others took off their sweats, Bird kept his on. Larry's edge was his size. He was a lot bigger than the others. He was 6 feet, 9 inches, and they averaged 6 feet, 3-1/2 inches. They shot three-pointers as jump shots. The taller Bird simply lofted them on their way. As the others tired, Larry got better. He hit 18 of his 25 shots in the final round. The three-point play is a Larry Bird specialty. In one nine-game stretch, he hit on 25 of 34. This is a 73.5 percent average. Many NBA players do not even shoot that well from the foul line.

The Celtics romped to their best team record, 67–15. Bill Walton played like Red Auerbach had hoped. The team looked ahead to the NBA playoffs. The Celtics wanted revenge. The public wanted to see Larry Bird and Magic Johnson play against each other again. Could Walton handle Kareem Abdul-Jabbar? As has happened before in the NBA, the matchup the public expected never took place. Houston would be the Celtics' opponent in the NBA Finals. Bill Fitch, the former Boston coach, was now in charge of Houston.

It was an up-and-down series. The Celtics won the first

two games in Boston but played poorly in on the road. They managed to squeeze out a 106–103 victory in the fourth game. However, the Rockets won Game 5 when another battle erupted. The Rockets' massive 7-foot, 4-inch Ralph Sampson threw an elbow at 6-foot, 1-inch Jerry Sichting. Like Larry Bird, Jerry was a hard-nosed player from the tough southern Indiana country. He challenged the towering Sampson. Both players were put out of the game. Even with the dominating Sampson banished, the Celtics floundered. It would take a trip back to Boston to end the series.

The Celtics were keyed up. They hammered the Rockets hard. "No one, except the Chicago Bears, has ever played a first quarter as aggressively as we did," said Coach K. C. Jones. The Celtics led by wide margins all through the game. They were ahead 55–38 at the half and won 114–97. Larry had a triple-double: 29 points, 11 rebounds, 12 assists. He also had three first half steals and was named MVP for the playoffs. A little later he learned he was voted MVP for the league for the third straight time. The Boston Celtics were again the champs. The dynasty could go on and on. However, Larry Bird had played in pain for a year and a half. What's more, the Celtics made a great pick in the 1986 college draft. They took Len Bias of Maryland. He had been at the Celtics' rookie free-agent camp the year before. There, Red Auerbach had learned how talented he was. He was like a Michael Jordan, only bigger. Larry Bird was so happy with the choice that he said he would come to the rookie camp himself. He would report a month early just to help Bias break in.

Then tragedy struck. Two days after the draft, Len Bias died of a cocaine overdose. He was twenty-two years old and partying in his dorm. The news shocked the sports world. The gifted young man who would have eventually replaced Larry Bird was another victim of drugs. In his autobiography, *Drive*, Larry Bird wondered: "How many great athletes have to die or have their careers ruined before they get the message?"

It was a more mature Larry Bird who spoke his mind. He changed his summer activities. He still found time to share with old friends but also began new business ventures. He had known of other superstars whose fortunes had been lost in bad deals. He still had the advice of "The Committee" to guide him. He liked the idea of owning a four-floor hotel in Terre Haute. It was called, "Larry Bird's Boston Connection." There were three different restaurants in the hotel. Larry's trophies and awards used to be kept in one of them. There was a gift shop with a line of Larry Bird and Boston Celtics items. T-shirts, replica jerseys with number 33, posters, etc., were sold there. Though successful for a while, the hotel and restaurants have since closed down.

Larry's hotel and three restaurants had given jobs to local people. He also owned a car sales business in the small town of Martinsville, Indiana. People used to drive hundreds of miles to have a Larry Bird sales decal on their car or pick-up truck.

During the 1986–87 season, the Celtics were almost unbeatable at home. They won 39 games and lost only 2. On the road, however, they had a losing record of 20–21. For the first time since the 1982–83 season, they did not lead the league in victories. The Lakers did. The Celtics managed to win the Eastern Conference championship. However, Los Angeles, with Magic Johnson as the MVP of the playoffs, won the NBA championship in six games. Magic Johnson also ended Larry Bird's hold on the league's Most Valuable Player award. After three straight years, Larry was upstaged by Magic.

The next season, the Lakers continued to be the NBA's dominant team. They became the first team since the Celtics of 1968 and 1969 to win back-to-back titles. The Celtics did not make the finals in 1988. The Detroit Pistons beat the Celtics in six games to become Eastern Conference champions. Basketball fans wondered if the reign of Larry Bird and the Boston Celtics was over. Had the Celtics' new dynasty ended? Would Larry Bird lead them back to the top? He would turn thirty during the coming season. How long could he continue to throw his body into game after game?

After winning their third Championship in the Bird Era, the Celtics selected Len Bias out of the University of Maryland. Most experts felt Bias would become a very good NBA player. The sports world was shocked when Bias died from a cocaine overdoes two days later.

Chapter
6

Always a Celtic

In the summer of 1988, Larry Bird's agent, Bob Woolf, negotiated a new contract with the Celtics. Boston had already reached the NBA cap on player salaries, so they were not able to offer Bird more money. Instead, his new contract called for a salary of $2.2 million and a nearly $5 million bonus just for signing the contract. It was agreed that Larry would put off receiving the bonus until 1991.

Bird was almost totally inactive during the 1988–89 season. His total season record amounted to eight preseason and six regular season games. He had been having some ankle trouble for the past few seasons. He would occasionally pull or strain his Achilles tendons. Stretching seemed to relax the muscles,

Looking on, Bird can only cheer his teammates in this game during December 1988. Bird missed most of that season with ankle and foot injuries.

but warm-up sessions were taking much longer. Eventually this condition worsened to the point where his ankle muscles would not stay loose and began to swell.

A CAT scan revealed that a spur (a bony growth) in Bird's right ankle had enlarged enormously. His doctor decided to surgically remove the spur. He predicted that Bird would be able to return to the court in March 1989. After surgery, Bird went through a strict routine of therapy, exercise, and stretching. He did whatever he could to get back into the lineup. He attempted to return in March, but his foot was not completely healed. He stayed out for the rest of the season.

Boston wound up with only 42 wins that season and finished in third place in the Atlantic Division of the Eastern Conference. They were blasted out of the quarterfinals three games to none by the Detroit Pistons. Detroit went on to win its first NBA championship, sweeping the defending champion Lakers in four straight. While recovering from surgery, Bird married his longtime girlfriend, Dinah Mattingly. The couple would eventually adopt two children, Connor and Mariah.

Larry Bird returned for the 1989–90 season eager to give the Celtics another winning campaign. But Boston was a new team from the one he left in 1988. K. C. Jones had been replaced by Jimmy Rodgers as the new Celtics coach. Danny Ainge had been traded to Sacramento. Brian Shaw left the Celtics to play in Italy. Tough, talented, and effective on the court, the older core of Bird, Parish, and McHale needed younger skilled players to back them up. But the backup players just were not there, and the regulars had to play longer in each game. As a result, Boston was wearing out its best players.

A high point for Bird in the season was his sinking of 71 consecutive free throws, coming close to the record of 78 set by Calvin Murphy. The Celtics finished in second place in the Atlantic Division, with 52 wins and 30 losses. On May 6, the Knicks knocked out Boston in the first round of playoffs, three games to two.

At the end of the 1989–90 season, Chris Ford replaced Jimmy Rodgers as Boston's coach. Ford had been a Celtics assistant coach for seven years. Under Coach Ford, the 1990–91 season began well for Bird and the Celtics. The team had made a number of changes in their style of play, including minimizing the use of the three-point shot. They focused on taking more high-percentage shots. Bird's position also changed. He was now power forward. But his chronic back problems forced him to miss 22 games. When he returned, it was rumored that he might announce his retirement at the end of the season.

In spite of Bird's injury, the Celtics won the Atlantic Division title with 56 wins and made it into the playoffs. Larry's fans hoped he would come back at 100 percent to play the Indiana Pacers in the first round.

Despite his sore back, Bird delivered a solid performance. Both Boston and Indiana played well and split the first four games. In the fifth and final game of the series, Larry hit his head on the floor as he dove for the ball. He made his way to the locker room, where the team doctor applied ice and did what he could for the bruise. In spite of the pain in his face, combined with his back injury, Bird performed incredibly. The Celtics took the final game, 124-121.

The Celtics now had to face the two-time defending champion Detroit Pistons. Bird sat out the first game due to his bad back, but came back in the second game. In Game 3, Boston handed Detroit a stunning 115–83 defeat. It was the Pistons worst home game in three years. Bird played 33 minutes in that game. He put in only 10 points, but offset that with 7 rebounds and 4 assists. The Celtics now had a two to one series lead, but their luck soon ran out. The next three games were won by Detroit, and the Celtics were out of the playoffs.

On June 8, 1991, Larry Bird walked out of New England Baptist Hospital. He had been there for surgery to relieve the back problems from the previous season. A bone fragment was removed from one of Bird's vertebrae. The fragment had put pressure on the nerve endings in the vertebrae, causing the pain in Larry's back. With no fragment, there was no pressure and therefore no pain. Dr. Arnold Scheller, the Celtics' team physician, said Larry's rehabilitation would include wearing a back brace and walking nearly ten miles each day.

Now plagued by injury, Larry Bird's time as the star of the Boston Celtics was winding down. Bird was forced to retire at the end of the 1991–92 season. That season he was limited to 45 games. Yet he averaged 20.2 points, 9.6 rebounds, and 6.8 assists per game.

Bird started his career in Boston as Rookie of the Year. At the time he retired, he was the NBA's all-time three-point field goal leader (that record has since been broken). Bird won three

The 1992 U.S. Men's Olympic Basketball Team is considered to be the best ever assembled. Bird was a member of this team, as was his old friend and rival, Magic Johnson.

NBA MVP Awards and led the Celtics to three NBA titles. He is a legend in basketball and in Boston, where he has joined the ranks of fellow Celtics greats Bill Russell and Bob Cousy. Boston loves the Celtics, and Larry Bird loves Boston. As Larry himself wrote, "I'll always be a Celtic."

Before retiring, Larry Bird decided to accept one more challenge. He became part of the 1992 U.S. Olympic basketball team. Known as the Dream Team, this was the first Olympic basketball team from the United States to feature pro athletes. Bird was one of many future Hall-of-Famers on the team, including Magic Johnson, Michael Jordan, and Charles Barkley. At the Summer Olympics in Barcelona, Spain, the Dream Team dominated. They won the gold medal with ease, defeating each of their eight opponents by an average of 44 points.

With the sight of the 1992–93 season approaching, Bird

held firm to his decision to retire from basketball. Although he would accept a role with the Celtics' organization, the position was very limited and resulted in Bird being able to live the retired life.

In 1997, Larry Bird became head coach of the Indiana Pacers. The team went 58–24 in his first season, and Bird won the Coach of the Year award. His team made the postseason in each of his three years as Pacers head coach. The team, though, was not able to capture a championship. The 1999–2000 Pacers team came the closest, falling to the Lakers in six games in the NBA Finals. After the season, Bird resigned from coaching.

Bird came back to the Pacers' organization as the team president in 2003. He then assumed full control of basketball operations after the 2007–08 season. During his time as president, the organization was mainly competitive in the Eastern Conference. The highlight for Bird came when he added another award to his mantle; the 2012 NBA Executive of the Year. He stepped down as team president at season's end.

One of the biggest highlights of Bird's life, though, occurred in 1998 when he was inducted into the Naismith Memorial Basketball Hall of Fame. In his enshrinement speech he said, "I wish my mother could be here. I know she's very proud looking down. She always told me, late in her life, a few years back, "for a blond-haired snotty little kid, you did very well, Larry. I'm very proud of you.""

Larry Bird gives his enshrinement speech as he is inducted into the Naismith Memorial Basketball Hall of Fame in 1998.

Career Statistics

College

Year	Team	GP	FG%	REB	PTS	AVG
1976–77	Indiana State	28	.544	373	918	32.8
1977–78	Indiana State	32	.524	369	959	30.0
1978–79	Indiana State	34	.532	505	973	28.6
TOTAL		94	.533	1,247	2,850	30.3

NBA

Year	Team	GP	FG%	REB	AST	STL	BLK	PTS	AVG
1979–80	Boston	82	.474	852	370	143	53	1,745	21.3
1980–81	Boston	82	.478	895	451	161	63	1,741	21.2
1981–82	Boston	77	.503	837	447	143	66	1,761	22.9
1982–83	Boston	79	.504	870	458	148	71	1,867	23.6
1983–84	Boston	79	.492	796	520	144	69	1,908	24.2
1984–85	Boston	80	.522	842	531	129	98	2,295	28.7
1985–86	Boston	82	.496	805	557	166	51	2,115	25.8
1986–87	Boston	74	.525	682	566	135	70	2,076	28.1
1987–88	Boston	76	.527	703	467	125	57	2,275	29.9
1988–89	Boston	6	.471	37	29	6	5	116	19.3
1989–90	Boston	75	.473	712	562	106	61	1,820	24.3
1990–91	Boston	60	.454	509	431	108	58	1,164	19.4
1991–92	Boston	45	.466	434	306	42	33	908	20.2
TOTAL		897	.496	8,974	5,695	1,556	755	21,791	24.3

Olympic Totals

Year	Team	GP	REB	AST	STL	BLK	PTS	AVG
1992	USA	8	30	14	14	1	67	8.4

More Info

Contact Larry Bird
c/o Boston Celtics
226 Causeway Street
Fourth Floor
Boston, MA 02114

Facebook: http://www.facebook.com/pages/Larry-
Bird-33/65370721100

On the Internet:
<http://www.basketball-reference.com/players/b/birdla01.
html>

<http://www.nba.com/history/players/bird_bio.html>

Index